A HOLY DREAD

A HOLY DREAD

R. A. VILLANUEVA

Alice James Books
NEW GLOUCESTER, MAINE
alicejamesbooks.org

© 2026 by R. A. Villanueva
All rights reserved
Printed in the United States

10 9 8 7 6 5 4 3 2 1

Alice James Books are published by Alice James Poetry Cooperative, Inc.

Alice James Books
Auburn Hall
60 Pineland Drive, Suite 206
New Gloucester, ME 04260
www.alicejamesbooks.org

Library of Congress Cataloging-in-Publication Data

Names: Villanueva, R. A. author
  http://id.loc.gov/authorities/names/n2014025815
  http://id.loc.gov/rwo/agents/n2014025815
Title: A holy dread / R.A. Villanueva.
Description: New Gloucester, Maine : Alice James Books, 2026.
Identifiers: LCCN 2025024305 (print) | LCCN 2025024306 (ebook) | ISBN
  9781949944860 trade paperback | ISBN 9781949944761 epub
Subjects: LCGFT: Poetry
  http://id.loc.gov/authorities/genreForms/gf2014026481
Classification: LCC PS3622.I49395 H65 2026 (print) | LCC PS3622.I49395
  (ebook) | DDC 811/.6--dc23/eng/20250623
LC record available at https://lccn.loc.gov/2025024305
LC ebook record available at https://lccn.loc.gov/2025024306

Alice James Books gratefully acknowledges support from individual donors, private foundations, and the Poetry Foundation (https://www.poetryfoundation.org).

Cover image: Carzen A. Esprela, Title: *Full House*, Medium: Acrylic on canvas, Size: 48" x 36," Year: 2022

for Xavier & Penelope—
Ever-brilliant, beloved

CONTENTS

Cusp   1

ONE

Mass   5
Lake View   7
Genesis 8:21   8
Sonnet 146   9
Electioneering   10
Ditching   11
Anthropocene   12
After Communion, late mass at St. Rose   13
The Anatomy Lesson   14
We open class with still images where   15
Paternoster   16

TWO

Epithalamion, Ithaka   19
Crown   21
Albumen   23
Saudade   25

Epithalamion, Memorial Day	26
Balikbayan	27
Archipelagic	28
Pareidolia	29
When Doves	31
Namesake	32
Tenebrae	34

THREE

Mirabilary
- *This dark is the same dark as when you close* — 37
- When she finds the moon tonight my daughter — 38
- When our son explains the mathematics — 39
- *I do not know how much longer I'll be* — 40
- On my deathbed I will remember this — 41
- Penelope holds a slice of apple — 42
- *Hallelujah* sings the choir and I — 43

FOUR

Devotional	47
Damnatio Memoriae	49
Annus Mirabilis	52
Book of Hours	54
For My Friends, In Reply to Your Question	56
Epithalamion Beginning with *The Tempest*	58

NOTES — 61
ACKNOWLEDGMENTS — 65

And all the things that happened with such sadness

these were the best days

...and I, still with my rough eyes, such holding

—**DIONNE BRAND,** *Nomenclature for the Time Being*

In,consummate,fatherhood,
To,count,not,heads,
But,fire.

—**JOSÉ GARCIA VILLA,** *Doveglion*

CUSP

A week home and my nephew has
now surprised me with this tooth he

places in my palm with the force
and grace of a small god. How he

and I are shocked by the white of
it—its root like Sanskrit chalks or

the cusps of ice shelves broken off
and loosed from the southern glaciers.

Of course there is blood. Of course I
teach him names for what each body

needs to give away. Of course I
tear at the sound of his mouth turned

to coins in the night. Blessed are all
these gifts and songs from our young skulls.

ONE

MASS

The world has always been ending, I
said. And you said: *Yes*. Today, half-lost

on the senderos, among its dry
brush and thorns, I hear my mother's voice

in the rocks—see in the rust plains and
lava bulbs and cairns stacked as markers

her cells massing upon her heart, lungs,
running riot along her sternum.

Soon, the nights of marrow-talk, of jabs
and the Seven Last Words. Serum nights

with viols, the Joyful Mysteries, thumbs
on decades falling asleep. I light

a match with the end of another,
warm poisons and gauze for the new year.

*

The world has always been ending, she
said. And I said: *Yes*. Today we walk
bearing hymnals and lilacs for the
gazebo green, for stairwells and chalks

drawn to mark the hem of a body.
We bring each place its dirge in the shape
of teeth, slugs, a tongue pressed to concrete,
its fugue scored for sirens and windpipes,

pellet guns and bells. We bless the blue
of this wide winter sky above our
city, for once. Let it mean more to
us than smoke, more than blood starved of air

beneath skin, more than anthems hollowed
or a field for stars, dying and dead.

*

The world has always been ending, he
said. And you said: *Yes*. Today they are
burning the names of the boys they are
shooting in the street. This because we—

and they—know ashes mean undone leads
and muzzles loosened, floodlights and flares,
eyes doused with milk. At the chapel for
vespers, a woman holds a globe she

has decked with poppies and birch-tar and
foil; her son colors in a book of
heralds and dragons, traces his palm.

Now: the Magnificat. Now: I am
down on my knees sure only that the
fires will come again and again.

LAKE VIEW

We save our best views for ghosts, line
the Palisades with candles and
memorial trinkets, crows stuffed
with sawdust and beads. Here is stone.

Here's a fist's worth of carnations
laid upon marble. Here is smoothed

granite, gin and passport candids,
rainwater to hold in a tin
etched with psalms. From the overlook

you catch fog giving way to Mt.
Baker, the egrets like knuckles

into the mouth of the after-
noon. What you feel is the sound of
your lungs heavy with wind, with prayer.

GENESIS 8:21

Satisfied, the gallows-man cracks
his back, checks his knots and hinges
for give and grease; he arranges

his tools. An aviary packed
full with vultures and fresh lilacs
hums nearby. A colonel cringes
at his portrait. Above: gauges

read pressures, rate ordnance, the bank,
slide of a turn; the pilots grin,
satisfied. Near sunrise a boy
will find a finch broken open,

its heart all glossy with the wings
of flies and, kneeling, he will eye
his father's belt, wipe dry his hands.

SONNET 146

The maggot dreams of the ear and
the wound, that welcome dark between

gauze and knee, cheek and skull, and
any open moment in the

body that will have it. The child-
fly wants a mouth to grow into,

a burn to salve, a heart to feed
on. It cheers for sugar and Job

and marrow. The maggot loves St.
Lazarus, though he walked away,

loves the warm cut banks of the chest.
When the maggot asks for wings, we

will answer with painted hands, eyes
beneath coins, a promise of graves.

ELECTIONEERING

Tomorrow we mind the moss
and empire grasses, will tend
to the tiger orchids hanging

from the hothouse rafters.
Today we bring ourselves
to matters of the crash and trill.

The arrowheads plead to be pulled
from the morning's quarry,
the plowshares clot with rust and

here I think of the soft sinew
which holds fast the heel
to the calf. I think of cataract

city-states minting their coins.
At our funeral, the bassoons
and oboes played "The Battle Hymn

of the Republic" in cut time.
The chorister promised songs
of paradise and disaster half-

averted: a house, broken free
of its caissons, kept aloft
on the wings of hawks.

DITCHING

Lately it appears the water
has been waiting for us to keep trying

to make it across. The rivers
and trenches glossed with light

know we are so relentless as to plan
for catastrophe, layering backup

upon reserve. A pilot could suffer
an aneurysm mid-flight and pass

quietly without panic in the cabin,
his crew collecting themselves to

drape him across the floor. A flock
of geese might cascade into our engines

and still the plane will float its way
downstream toward the Battery.

ANTHROPOCENE

Lower Peninsula, I leave
you these nickels, this glassine of
sand from the forward line. I leave
you photos of her in the snow

in Romulus. The Lord said: *And
so render unto Caesar his
tithes, his cedars and calves.* The Lord
said: *Blessed are those who wash their robes.*

She wrote: *You were gone. I had no
way of knowing how you'd come back.*

Sault Ste. Marie, I give to you
what's left of my throat and these tusks
brushed with shellac. Here is an urn.
Trust the ashes inside are mine.

AFTER COMMUNION, LATE MASS AT ST. ROSE

and my parents are laughing about their
graves again. Dad passes his offering
envelope down, points to paired drawings in
felt-tip pen. The first maps trees, paths, and where

to find Mom, swooping cursive taking care
to note *Here I am*. Another: Route 10,
landmarks, lights and turn-by-turn directions
for birthday visits. In the car later

they knock at the windshield. We drive beside
the front gates and I refuse to look through
or touch a pamphlet which lists all you might

save now with family plots. No space left
to park, so we circle, then leave. Lunar
gardening on the news. And floods. A lost child.

THE ANATOMY LESSON

Copenhagen Zoo, 9 February 2014

The children circle Marius,
watch as his hide is peeled back from
around his forelegs, watch haunches

and neck opened to expose bone.
His keeper speaks of rifles, wild
dogs' jaws, and acacia thorns, points:

Those tigers care only for blood;
these hyenas only for rot.
A girl plays with her spit. Somewhere,

a truck hauling garlic erupts
into a bus; a mother's heart

fills with water; an armistice
falls dead. And what of mercy? *Harm*
is the norm. The doom should not jam.

WE OPEN CLASS WITH STILL IMAGES WHERE

      by the thousands above Costa Brava
starlings flock and tumble, swirl in answer

      to some unseen danger, their looping dark
against that bonfire sky, shifting: a
      haze of wings and panicked rally cries, a
spiral galaxy, bodies together

      becoming chorus, then a shadow bird
my students say reminds them of tidal
      pools or smoke, the states of matter. I spell

murmuration and listen as they write
      murder in their notes instead. It is May.

We are not safe. But we'll go when drill bells
      sound—will play invisible, cut our lights,
shut the blinds, block every way out and wait.

PATERNOSTER

        that night   a wreck   a face   her teeth
beneath a wheel   her dress   your grief

        that night   a field   of deer   a breath
the sound   of bells   a child   to grieve

        a name   a womb   to fill   with glass
and dye   its knots   to frame   our grief

        has mass will bloom   will burn   like gas
will smoke   a harbor   alight   with grief

        tonight   a show   for bricks   a tithe
of brass   and dirt   a spine   to grieve

        to run   each street   to church   a raft
of ash   raise high   the beams   for grief

TWO

EPITHALAMION, ITHAKA

Tell of the bride girl thinking of thread work,
dreaming of coronals, eagles and ducks,
staring out to the sea. Morning after
morning touching her throat, counting the veins
of her wrists, bracing for earthquakes. Sing of
snail shells dipped in wine, in boiled figs, stacked in
the silence of a bedchamber painted
with wax. That we know oracles gladly
lie will not keep us from asking, so she
asks into the dregs, into the blush
and warp of sunrise: *What will become of me?*

     And the Everything replies with corners
amid omens: dead bees, three torn veils, rain;
handmaids dressing burns, laughing into cups.

Past a grove of olive trees, hemlock, copse
of poplar, cypress—past the tall fires
and offering stones, the oxen and cliff
face and potters' kilns, look: his stables and
storerooms of lavender, axe heads, wild goat
cured with thyme. See, there: his oarsmen flexing
their legs, oiling their backs. See: ships' masts lashed
with laurels, carved with owls, the pitch, thick, dark-
growing-dark upon each hull and the sails,
broad, blooming like a field of clouds falling
in love with the tide. Down the corridor,

someone is peeling citrus, sharpening
their knives. Someone tunes strings, readies the dye
for feathers while she hums, braiding her hair.

To the thrumming stars, the scrim of daybreak
she takes her name. From her father's mouth, her
mother's chest she lifts it and breathes free each
syllable as if weaving in smoke who
she was before their promises, before
his oaths—his vows and signet rings, his hands
around hers like a shroud.   *Penelope—*

she calls, remembering how these last weeks
she would wade in the low reeds listening
for the weightless drift of wings, awake to
gods of her own making, a universe
luminous and spinning, reaching out its
voice to meet hers without secrets or grief,
only tenderness beyond surrender.

Beyond the wrecks, beyond her grace and faith
wound true then unraveling in turns, tears,
battlements, arrowheads and the harbor
watch, beyond porticoes and spiderwebs,
beyond daughter or queen, mother or wife—

        Penelope, alone, counts juniper
berries, presses them down with her thumb, tests
a smile. Dare to imagine her happy,

alive among all-trembling miracles,
bright with unruly gifts. Soon the phantoms
and thieves will circle. Soon the carrion

birds and soothsayers' drums and every small
catastrophe laced with joy. But for now
she keeps dear her heart, holds it far from dawn.

CROWN

To hear it their way we wanted
ships' holds, fields of tobacco and

cane, canneries reeking of cod,
whale, prawns to devein; we wanted

more sand to die in; we wanted
fingernails worn to the quick and

carrion crows' songs, borderland
raids, boots on the ground. We *wanted*

this, they say. We asked for it
with our hardened necks, our cakes, our

unpronounceable names. *Why must
each damned lake and bird of the air*

need altar and mouth, horn and dance?
—they call out to us with fire.

*

They called out to us with fires
before posing for photographs,
arranging each shadow with care—

each child's dead stare, bangle, and half-
touch a corona to circle
missionary men, or their wives.

They called out to us with charnel
work and missals, cinnabar mines

to dig in service of the Crown

and cross. What's cut from the portrait
is the cordillera, the sun
warming our flints, coals, a piglet

run through and this girl searching for
her son, his jawbone bruised, tender.

ALBUMEN

With the name of your first child your mother
speaks of her brothers, stillborn, laid to rest

in the family plot. How the southern
provinces flooded full those seasons, fat

with novenas and rain. We look away.
You kiss his face, open your gown to nurse,

ask for someone to braid your hair. The boy
has lungs like bellows so you make a place

for his lips. Then, there is quiet. We stare
up at the TV, where detectives trawl

a shore front, trace a body with lights, bare
its bruises and cuts. You close your eyes, tell

of his birth in water warm to your waist.
We pray: *Holy Family. O Holy Ghost.*

*

Each of us raised by a family of ghosts
and masks and talking gods. That the Good
Lord knew His mother dreamt nightly of boys

cut down for Him—held their voices inside
Her—is certain. And that we know we have
stolen air from those we love is sure. In

albumen prints of Hopi dancers, the
men all grasp snakes in their hands or teeth, sing
for rain with rattles and whips. Faces flush

with clay or feldspar, the sky behind them
is parchment. They tap feathers to the earth.

Think here of incense, noise, covenant hymns—
how Palm Sundays we spent the liturgy
knotting crosses from branches, swords from leaves.

*

Not lime or bleach, but oil and spore; knives, sword-
sharp, left to the sink, catching rust. Each day

it proves more difficult to shrug away
the cracks in the moulding, the clots of hair

in the drain. So I say *I love you more
than everything*, and mean *You cannot die*

before I do. I mean *Every joy
we have nests within these bodies' finer*

rots. According to the numbers, we don't
have time. Glaciers are losing ground, white smoke

blossoms from a caldera, and your womb
grows tired of waiting for us to talk.

What else do we have? I love you more than
all this. You cannot die before I do.

SAUDADE

Yes now, like you, I wonder: where
is the patron saint of exiles
and far districts, this prefecture
of salt licks, pollen? Of alleys

blue with plaques? And who among those
martyrs gives the nieces we have
yet to hold close our faces to
learn, our names to try? Who will halve

our pills for us, heat the bacon
fat, steep the tea? Everywhere wine
and moss. Everywhere fog. *The wrecks
of ships around the Whitefish Point*

and bodies the lake won't give back,
you say. *Like that—a love like that.*

EPITHALAMION, MEMORIAL DAY

Forecasts say prepare for rain, so you will—
will keep at the ready tarp and cord, tents

and candles. And you will drink to the gulls
circling and the May sun high above rocks

ahead of you which promise everything
will be just fine. That this is for good. That

you are the answer to Suzhou gardens
lit by the moon, a caldera sunset,

bunkers off the coast at dawn. Allow them
their quiet warships and wreaths. You have wine

in sight of Saturn, peony and drum
and pearl. Hold now to the sound of a life

you've waited your life for. Yours is this blue
to swim under, this sky to leap into.

BALIKBAYAN

Name a brother's son Pterodactyl, hold
him to the sky and watch the boy compare

your face to his father's—shape of the eyes,
folds of a mouth. When he brings his forehead

to meet yours, see the mark, there, a soft red,
same as the bruise between your brother's eyes

(gone now) left by a fastball to his face
that summer on the front lawn. You told Dad

it was nothing and hoped he'd miss the seams,
the blood just below the skin. Years ago,

in Batangas, Grandpa wanted to see
the ocean, so you cut his hair, took him

to the coast and sat him on the sand. You
spoke of salt and plums; he practiced your names.

ARCHIPELAGIC

Not vinegar. Not acid. Not
sugarcane pressed to mortar by
fist, but salt: salt, the home taste; salt,
the tide; salt, the blood. Not Holy

Ghost, but a saint of coral come
to life in the night crossing a
field of brambles and thorns, the camps
of pirates beat back to the bay

with hornets. Not Santo Niño.
And not a belt of storms, but this:
girls singing, an avocado
in each open palm, courting doves;

a moth drawn to the light of our
room you take to be your father.

PAREIDOLIA

When the new year came with whole flocks of doves
and jackdaws falling dead upon the fields,

landfills and roofs blackened with wings; the lakes
silvered with drumfish, their bellies bloated,

eyes thickened to milk. The ministers sang
of seals and omens, sang of prophecies

above tambourines and horns. For starlings
they cried, for spiders flooded into trees,

for the quakes and fires. Last night the moon
hovered like a scimitar over an East

River bloodied by the air. We took planes
for constellations, named strobes for comets;

we watched a crowd kneel before a hollow,
calling: *Mary, Our Lady of Sorrows.*

*

They call: *Beata Maria Virgo
Perdolens, pray for us,* divining shapes

from knots weathered open, bark crowned with sap.
They bow *Salve, Regina* at the foot

of this tree flanked by lilies and find—clothed
in mantle of blue—the Virgin atop

scars in the trunk. Hers is the form they hope
we see first, an image we know we won't

hold holy or miraculous. Picture
this: what appears here is something of the

body. Not Her eyes or mouth dressed with stars,
not hands in coronal loops, but that part

of his wife St. Joseph would never see,
that place touched once by the Holy Spirit.

WHEN DOVES

At the columbarium dug
by hand, a man points to where rock
doves would be brought to nest, their eggs

tended by priests, and the cave locked
at sundown, guarded by hired
knives. The flock meant meat for the dry

times; saltpeter; yolks needed to bind
portraits to walls, to raise a sky
gilded with violets and myrrh.

Tonight, my mother paints her nails
black—a shade she names "Dark Matter."
She numbers what's left of her cells,

tells us of this burning inside
her knees, laughs a promise to fight.

NAMESAKE

By daybreak the two had been locked
together for hours on the riverbank
among bulrushes and moss flowers,
struggling, some translations say,
or *grappling*, knuckles braided,
wrists bruised, their bodies become
a dovetail joint where a windpipe
might disappear in the glow
and salt of a bicep. Choke hold,
half nelson, laughter and necks'
shake and parry—imagine the funk
and rumble of their waltz:
that Jacob vs. his God, or vs.
the face of his God; or that
Jacob folding into a stranger's
outstretched wings, the story,
as ever, ending in blessings
and one hip pulled clean
from its socket. Such is the algebra
of certain parables that we
can cast other rivals
for the fray: this Jacob
fighting his faith or, yes, *wrestling*
the specters of fatherhood; this
Jacob and the glare of Peckham
streetlamps, staring down
train tables and yet another horizon
just north of home; Jacob chasing
invoices from the Queen,
or bike thieves making off
with new wheels; this Jacob's flex
against the bindings of language,

of acronyms, of history, of
how boys too often worship fists
instead of syllables or
the weight of a lover's heart
in their hands. In Gauguin's
Vision after the Sermon, perhaps
what matters most isn't the soft
knot of blue in the upper
reaches of the canvas, or
the staggering radiance
of the clearing where Jacob and
what we take to be an angel
seize each other, but
a gathered congregation,
their faces lit by what promises
to cleave Jacob open
but never does, their eyes
shut, humbled by calamity
and its tenderness, sure now
that they know: devotion,
what it means to praise, to love,
to survive love and the divine.

TENEBRAE

Shame the light for what grief it brings
the eye, even shut: radiant
the slaughterhouse; phosphorous shells

bright, fed on bone and wedding sweets.
Damn the light—damn the glow of their
sirens, their liturgy of flag

to kerosene, torch to altar
and crossbeam. Praise instead the night,
its starless, basilica void.

Praise the black of ventricles, new
blood. Praise his holy ruckus and
jolt—this boy as echo, shadow,
high-relief. Glory be his mouth,
warm on the soft dark of her breast.

We care about each other so militantly, with such softness, that we exhaust ourselves, and then record, in the resonance of our slightly opened mouths, the sound of that, in the absence of the enemy that we keep making.

—**FRED MOTEN,** "hand up to your ear"

THREE

MIRABILARY

THIS DARK IS THE SAME DARK AS WHEN YOU CLOSE

your eyes, I whisper to our son while he

    catches his breath. It is well past midnight

and he will not describe the face of what

    he fights to unsee. By his feet, the green

glow of a nightlight retreats into blue,

    slips softly to red. Above his bed: notes

we once had time to tape onto the latch

    of his lunchbox, flights of origami

swans, throwing stars and fortune tellers. When

    your turn comes to lie beside him, this is

the bridge he's set to repeat: *Always an*

    angel, never a god—and so you hold

him close like a saint shadowed by the axe,

    cradling her own haloed head in her hands.

WHEN SHE FINDS THE MOON TONIGHT MY DAUGHTER

grabs my arm and narrates her happiness,
explaining how *all that sky up there* cuts
the moon in two like a sliced grape then

pulls open her bookbag, digs through her snacks
to find one to hold up to the dark, juice
running the curve of her chin—

WHEN OUR SON EXPLAINS THE MATHEMATICS

of my birthday, he stands, charts bonds and tens,
figures my years amount to 33
minus 3, plus 7, then 5 and 3
—again we are taken by the circuits
of his mind glowing as he imagines

the distances between us. Here we
are among his diagrams talking nerve
cells and the fading color of our hair,
what animal shapes we make of the clouds—

I DO NOT KNOW HOW MUCH LONGER I'LL BE

alive in this world, Mom is telling us
while rubbing behind her knees, while pressing
her temples. When making eggs for us, she

spoons hot oil across the yolks, passes plates
of rice, minced onion, fistfuls of salt then
glances to her clutch of pills, tracks
the color of her veins. She winces. She

carries. She wishes for everyone she
loves to swim together before the end.

I remember asking which language her
dreams move in. I remember: her hair like
a hall of smoke, tape unspooled from cassettes;
pollen on the keys of an untuned piano—

ON MY DEATHBED I WILL REMEMBER THIS

afternoon   My son on the floor of the
    gallery in the sunlight through the blinds,
faint shadows of a vitrine and on the

    facing wall: portraits   in burnished frames, all
their soft expressions   My wife, there, braving

    the cold with our daughter whose screams of joy
filled the atrium as she unfastened
    herself, leapt *Help me!* (which sounded at first

like *Honey!*)   Those were the days when they still
    snuck into bed between us   for solace,
for certain calm to brace their stretching bones—

PENELOPE HOLDS A SLICE OF APPLE

in each hand as the celebrant recounts

for us *the inheritances of sin*

then touches his thumb to balsam and oil,

her chest, the crown of her skull. She does not

take easily to the water, cries

out for us, kicking free—

HALLELUJAH SINGS THE CHOIR AND I

reach low   *Hallelujah*   while our daughter
snores on my shoulder, drools onto my neck

What dreams I can remember are the dreams
that frighten me most   Ice and hairline cracks

on the wings near takeoff, a white-gray mass
among contrast studies, nurses leaving

us, tightening their smiles   There is
a theater blistered by bomblets, a school-

yard scattered with phones, peaches and triage
tents   There are letters left in the desert

—and acres of cypress burning   Patmos
and the Mournes, wellheads and the abyssal

plains of the Gulf burning still   I know this
child will learn to curse the sound of my voice

FOUR

DEVOTIONAL

I am writing this
to you among these
strangers on the 2
train because you
sometimes laugh
that you would love
for me to write
a poem for you—and
not that other kind
of thing I often do,
that elliptical, art-
thick wandering
that delays *I*
love you
for well-after
the spectacle, or
the heart-fraught
rhyme, the cave
cathedral, a
painted scroll
bound with locks
of hair. How easy
it is to lose track
of the truth,
the marrow of you
and I together
all these beautiful
years. *I love*
you I am tapping
with my thumbs
as someone's grandmother
snores beside me
clutching her grocery
bags, a weathered

Bible. *I love you*
I am saying now
in my head, opening
my eyes to find
myself looking
face-to-face
at a child
eating a corn muffin,
punching his
sister in the arm.
Last night, in the fog
of a fever and stress
headaches all I
wanted was soup,
its slivers of roast
pork, its green
onions and the warmth
of broth in my chest.
And last night you
filled our last clean bowl
and held it in a towel,
touched my forehead,
and said *Here you go.*
At this stop, I transfer
to the 1, which slides
local up into the Bronx
for what feels
like hours. Let me tell you
again without ornament
and for only you
and I to hear
in my voice
I love you.

DAMNATIO MEMORIAE

    "I shall create! If not a note, a hole.
    If not an overture, a desecration."

        —Gwendolyn Brooks, "Boy Breaking Glass"

A hollow-cast bronze
of an emperor stands
fast to a makeshift plinth
unburied from a ditch
behind an orchard, his
forehead split, temples

hammered-in, his jaw thrown
to the crucible blazes—& see
a clutch of saints now
polychrome fog adorned
with the many instruments
of martyrdom, rising

up tabernacle walls lit
by candles rendered
from animal fat, all eyes
gone, all their mouths
scratched clean away by fang
or grit. Because: damnation.

Because: oblivion &
jubilation & rapture.
Because this forgetting
demands the brutal magic
of rage. I confess
these days I hold dear

to such reckonings
—& to the sight of flags
cut from their masts, or
as embers underfoot
in capital parkyards &
to word of statues unbolted,

tarps, cranes, generals
of zinc bound for rats
& rock salt, riders pulled
down in the dead of night
to whistles & vigils
& bricks. Tomorrow,

our flight home
lands on a runway north
of arrivals, will rumble
toward border control
& its arrows, cordons
to snake us past mute

slideshows of meadowlarks,
musket fire, a choir's
salutes beside the last
launch of Atlantis. There,
in full view of guards &
exits, we walk to that space

marked for heads of state
& find again this dying
to tear at their portraits,
to hit back, crack plaques,
barrel through mirrors
& memorials—all this daring,

though, kept inside, kept
quiet. Not blasphemy or
sacrilege enough & far
from actual defiance, we
give them only our eyeballs
rolling gently in their

orbits, daydreams marching
around the empty theaters
of our skulls—& yet look:
my son is here in my arms,
beyond passport checks &
customs scans now, a riot

of laughter lunging at
those photos, wanting,
it seems, to prime fists or
to drum his knuckles
against their grins or smear
both palms bright with spit

& wet with sick across
the glass. I swear I know
this means nothing, but
imagine: his hands'
unspeakable mess visible
to the whole terminal,

a kind of beckon, a slurry
inviting each body to join
in their own way, so we
might face together these
restless monsters we have
made for ourselves.

ANNUS MIRABILIS

From the shallows our son watches me play
dead. He sits on river rocks chucking sand,
burying strawberries while I float down-
stream, breath wound bright in the gut, a body

both here and of other waters. The day
he was born, midwives touched your face, your hands,
measured nerve and pulse, dripped saline along
your thigh, numbered blades—their ceremony

for the first cuts, before swaddling blankets,
fever syrups, bath time and mud. These are
places the boy is ticklish: lunette

of the earlobe   kneecaps   madrigal fat
of his belly   collarbone   toes. These words
he knows, but will not say: *yes*   *horse*   *sleep*   *white*.

*

Again the boy cries himself hoarse
as we sing through these hours right

before dawn. First the alphabet,
then "Twinkle, Twinkle Little Star,"

then "The Great Pretender." Our words
like foxes, like milk teeth. We can't

hold him quiet. His body must,
they say, learn now about hunger,

about being alone. So we
hum and *shhh* into the yellow

bruise of Sunday, melodies the
shape of bluets and yearlings, blood

pudding and this worry, this awe
we have no name for—

*

When he asks, make no mention of those names
we saved for the children we lost—his ghost
siblings, their phantom initials. Of tests

and lemongrass, nettle leaf and sharps, forms
in triplicate, clinics painted with lambs,
comets, maps to nerve meridians, hearts:

say nothing. Never speak of that quiet
after the kicking stopped. Believe in time
he'll learn our cells betray each miracle
and wild conundrum they're coded to bear.

      If he needs an answer, give him morning
mass off W. 16th: how aisle and chancel
roared with lilies and cornets; how we dared
a new unknown to find us, there, in song.

BOOK OF HOURS

Lake-deep black of night and no song we sing
will do. After pillow forts, Minotaur

lullabies, glow-in-the-dark starfighters,
shadow animals' chomp and gallop, wing-

flap and pearl—between flood tide and lightning
bloom, our son keeps awake and smiles, rhymes *storm*

with *remember*, *bird* with *brother* with *Earth*.
I kiss the rise of your hip bone, the fringe

of your dearest scar. From someplace inside
the stillness we hear him yawn, then this voice

sounding out the murk, whispering for us
to swear we will never not be alive

together: *I wished for flowers and good dreams,
but monsters find us now. Can you save me?*

*

      And still we save our mornings for *Monster
Time!* His laughter bearing a frill of horns,
    a war dance smirk of play-fangs and talons.
Ode to tackles, leaps, my son kissing where

    small hands draw blood, the welter of tigers
he growls into at will, his coelacanths

      conjured from bells. Ode to the boy's thousand
magnets and butterflies, his gown of sharks.

      After their baths, the children ask to talk
about extinction—about what cannot
      come back and why, about soot and fossils.

We listen to the ambulance corps barrel
      down off-ramps toward fireworks. We take
sight of roses, padlocks, masks. We count mouths.

*

Dear Nethermead   Dear hillrise swans' locket
of wings, felled oaks to ring the Lullwater

edge   Dear daughter   Dear gladness defiant,
rebel mouth of honeybees and mirrors,

paper cranes and lemons—& when I reach
spoons to you we open *ahhh* like kindred

passerines   We meet eyes: you, sabertooth
cub, and me, the evening kill graced in red—

Insomniac joy   Our holy dread   If
prayer meant anything, I'd beg forgiveness

for what's to come, for these ruins we gift
bedecked with embers and pomegranates,

for each grim atom of the inferno
we could not hope to endure without you

FOR MY FRIENDS, IN REPLY TO YOUR QUESTION

We are making it through, yes,
but barely. What we have now
is at the least an everyday—
some bewildering dance where we
keep time with each other. My son
has chosen a corner of our street
where we're meant to track
the neighborhood's drifting
into spring: he watches a vine
creep along the brick face,
notes with pastels and gel pens,
its roots clawing the mortar,
a lone bumblebee in its fat orbit
around nearby blossoms. He tends
to his own carnations in a jar
of dye and water, sketches
an experiment to test if color
will disappear into the air. *Nothing
is ever all-gone*, he says, gently
drowning a small cactus
he carried from the bodega
before it shuttered for good. Later,
he will list the names of everyone
we miss. Later, he will sing
"Happy Birthday" to a cousin
across the Palisades, to an uncle
three stops away on the F,
to a family friend out west
as we gather by the light
of screens, around the dinner table
at a house my parents hope
to give away. We leave
Brooklyn for here—this lawn

I had to mow in the summer,
this backyard where Grandpa
nursed tomatoes and green beans,
where my brother and I
pressed rocks into the earth,
flicked pill bugs onto their backs.
I tried to tell my son those stories,
but he was chalking the driveway,
throwing tennis balls at windows,
pouring bubble solution
into flower beds. No one
has slept here in months
and I've spent these first hours
home paging through albums
while my daughter rolls
among the quilts and pillows
of the living room. She laughs
when I take her hands to cup
them to my ears, when I tickle
the ridges of her ribcage, when
we call her name with soft,
percussive notes, whisper *boom
boom boom* in triplet. You
could never imagine my hair
this long. Every photograph
and keepsake sits covered in dust.

EPITHALAMION BEGINNING WITH *THE TEMPEST*

Because Ariel speaks of a king's son,
his boats aflame, crying, *Hell is empty,*
and all the devils are here, I ask my
son to tell me about love. He chalks crowns

and rockets across newsprint, draws wolves, rain
clouds, an owlet, says, *You love me—and my*
mama. I love triceratops.   We try

these mornings to bring ourselves to trust in
the sound of our breathing over the spent
shells and laughter, the incandescent head-
stones. We hold our bodies as covenant

enough—and vow *Yes*, promise *Yes*. Despite
every havoc we still sing of orchids
to ribbon, opals and bones' swallowed light.

NOTES

CUSP
This poem is for Kima and Tahjair.

MASS
Before these sonnets were brought together as an unnumbered sequence, they were conceived with these titles—and dedications:

1. Kyrie
2. Requiem (for Tamir Rice, Akai Gurley, and Eric Garner)
3. Dies Iræ (for Michael Brown)

THE ANATOMY LESSON
On 9 February 2014, keepers at the Copenhagen Zoo euthanized a healthy giraffe named Marius. They then butchered and fed Marius to the lions. As reported by *The Guardian*: Marius's death was "followed by his dissection in front of a large crowd, including fascinated-looking children, prompting outrage and protests around the world."

The final italicized lines adapt phrases from the novel *Pnin* by Vladimir Nabokov.

WE OPEN CLASS WITH STILL IMAGES WHERE
At the heart of this poem is "A Bird Made of Birds," a 2019 performance and talk by Sarah Kay.

PATERNOSTER
Originally sparked by a conversation with Janine Joseph's students at Weber State University in 2016, this attempt at a ghazal hopes to be in dialogue with "Obligations 2" by Layli Long Soldier.

ALBUMEN
This family of sonnets is an ekphrastic response to images and art from the collection of the Peabody Essex Museum in Salem, Massachusetts. In particular: *Andaman Island, Papuans, 1869,* an albumen print by Samuel Bourne and Charles Shepherd, and *Bontoc Woman, Philippines, ca. 1903,* a gelatin silver print by Charles Martin.

SAUDADE
As with the Catalan, "enyorança," and the Welsh, "hiraeth," it is often said there is no exact way to render the Portuguese, "saudade," into English. *Impossible, yes*—a woman after a poetry reading once needed me to understand—*because saudade is here and here and here.* She hummed those italics, pressing upon her ribcage, her waist, the insides of her wrists. She meant: *My heart and my guts and veins.* As if the yearning of "saudade" wasn't something to translate into precise terms, but was, instead, something inherited, carried, felt in the body.

EPITHALAMION, MEMORIAL DAY
This poem is for Patty and Jonathan, Christina and Chris, and Jennifer.

BALIKBAYAN
This poem is for Ryan and RR, Dad and Grandpa.

In Tagalog, the compound word, "balikbayan," melds a verb with a noun: the combination of "balik" (to return) and "bayan" (homeland) has become a name given to Filipinos who travel back to the Philippines after living abroad.

PAREIDOLIA

"Pareidolia" refers to the human mind's capacity for imagining meanings and perceiving forms in random patterns, or naturally-occurring phenomena.

In July 2012, a tree at the corner of 60th Street and Bergenline Avenue in West New York, New Jersey, became a pigrimage site, drawing hundreds of visitors a day. The faithful believed that the appearance of Our Lady of Guadalupe was a sign from heaven.

NAMESAKE

This poem is for Jacob Sam-La Rose.

TENEBRAE

This poem was envisioned as a response to the UK's National Poetry Day in 2015. The theme for celebrations and projects that year was "light."

MIRABILARY

The title of this poem is indebted to the writing of Anne Boyer. A "mirabilary" is "one who, or a work which, narrates wonderful things," or "one who writes of wonders."

THIS DARK IS THE SAME DARK AS WHEN YOU CLOSE

This sonnet ends with lyrics from the song "Not Strong Enough" by the band boygenius.

DEVOTIONAL

This poem is for Jennifer.

DAMNATIO MEMORIAE
Translated from Latin, "damnatio memoriae" means "condemnation of memory." It describes the practice of defacing memorials, statuary, or grave monuments to erase, or symbolically negate, a person's existence.

FOR MY FRIENDS, IN REPLY TO YOUR QUESTION
This poem is after Safia Elhillo.

ANNUS MIRABILIS
This poem is for Xavier.

The title is Latin for "year of miracles."

BOOK OF HOURS
This poem is for Penelope.

The phrase, "our holy dread," is inspired by a moment from Mary Ruefle's *Madness, Rack, and Honey*. In her essay, "On Fear," she reflects on Julian of Norwich's *Revelations of Divine Love*: "And the fourth form of dread is 'born of reverence,' the holy dread with which we face that which we love most, or that which loves us the most."

And the coda echoes Italo Calvino's *Invisible Cities* (trans. William Weaver): "The inferno of the living is not something that will be; if there is one, it is what is already here, the inferno where we live every day, that we form by being together. There are two ways to escape suffering it. The first is easy for many: accept the inferno and become such a part of it that you can no longer see it. The second is risky and demands constant vigilance and apprehension: seek and learn to recognize who and what, in the midst of the inferno, are not inferno, then make them endure, give them space."

EPITHALAMION BEGINNING WITH *THE TEMPEST*
This poem is for Paige and Kaveh.

ACKNOWLEDGMENTS

Boundless gratitude goes to the editors and staff of the following literary journals and projects. Their generosity, care and belief in this work—through all its shifts and forms—means the world.

Ambit: "For My Friends, In Reply to Your Question"
American Poetry Review: "Mass"
swamp pink (formerly *Crazyhorse*): "Genesis 8:21"
The Common: "Electioneering," "Albumen," "Epithalamion, Memorial Day," and "Pareidolia"
Five Points: "Cusp"
Guernica: "Tenebrae"
Iterant: "Devotional"
Mānoa: A Pacific Journal of International Writing: "We open class with still images where"
The Margins: "Ditching"
Ploughshares: "Book of Hours" and "Epithalamion Beginning with *The Tempest*"
Poems In Which: "Paternoster"
Poetry: "Sonnet 146"
Poetry London: "*Hallelujah* sings the choir and I"
The Poetry Review: "Anthropocene"
Prac Crit: "Saudade"

The Rialto: "Namesake"
The Rumpus: "Damnatio Memoriae"
The Sewanee Review: "After Communion, late mass at St. Rose"
TAYO Literary Magazine: "Lake View"
wildness: "The Anatomy Lesson" and "Balikbayan"
The Wolf: "Crown"

"Epithalamion, Ithaka" was originally commissioned for *Bedtime Stories for the End of the World*, a podcast created and produced by Eleanor Penny and Tom MacAndrew.

"Saudade" was Highly Commended for the Forward Prizes and anthologized in *The Forward Book of Poetry 2017*.

"Archipelagic," "When Doves," "*This dark is the same dark as when you close*," and "Annus Mirabilis," were featured by the Academy of American Poets as part of their Poem-a-Day series.

Praise to friends, mentors and comrades—gracing stages and pages, in the groupchats and beyond: Hanif Abdurraqib, Helene Achanzar, Kaveh Akbar, Hala Alyan, Eloisa Amezcua, Romalyn Ante, Raymond Antrobus, Gina Apostol, Marissa Aroy, Fatimah Asghar, Hossannah Asuncion, Gabrielle Bates, Rhoni Blankenhorn, Malika Booker, Victoria Adukwei Bulley, Troy Cabida, Anne Carson & Robert Currie, Paul Hlava Ceballos, Sumita Chakraborty, Marianne Chan, Jennifer Chang, Cathy Linh Che, Kayo Chingonyi, Noah Arhm Choi, Anthony Cody, Meg Day, Safia Elhillo, Inua Ellams, Shira Erlichman, Tarfia Faizullah, Laurel Flores Fantauzzo, Jumoké Fashola, Melissa Ferrer Civil, Aracelis Girmay, Rachel Eliza Griffiths, Will Harris, Marwa Helal, Richie Hofmann, Sarah Howe, Ishion Hutchinson, K. Iver, Mira Jacob, Janine Joseph, Sarah Kay, Devin Kelly, Crystal Hana Kim, Abena Koomson-Davis, Eugenia Leigh, Paige Lewis, Kabel Mishka Ligot, Rachel Long, Éireann Lorsung, Ricardo Alberto Maldonado, Dante Micheaux, Cynthia Miller, John Murillo, Angel Nafis, Aimee Nezhukumatathil, Nita Noveno, José Olivarez, Darius Phelps, Julia Phillips, Patrick Rosal & Mary Rose Go, Levi Rubeck, Nicole Sealey, Omar Sakr, Sam Sax, Chet'la Sebree, Solmaz Sharif, Beowulf Sheehan, Eric Smith, Jayson P. Smith, Yomi Ṣode, Lara Stapleton, Bianca Stone, Toni Stuart, Ruth Sutoyé, Dujie Tahat, Obi Taswell, Jack Underwood, Kelly Sue White, Maya Williams,

Eric Yip...& yes praise and reckless thanks to you.

Glory be to the indomitable communities, collectives, and classrooms that illuminate what matters most: the Asian American Writers' Workshop; Barbican Young Poets and Jacob Sam-La Rose; Brooklyn Poets; my colleagues and students at ECFS; Kundiman; Liz's Book Bar and Maura Cheeks; Out-Spoken, Anthony Anaxagorou and Joelle Taylor; Poetry School (UK); Randolph College, Gary Dop and Chris Gaumer; Sarah Lawrence College, Paige Ackerson-Kiely and Maddie Mori; SupaDupaFresh, Mahogany L. Browne & Adam Falkner & Jive Poetic & Rico Frederick & Jon Sands; the Constance Saltonstall Foundation for the Arts and Lesley Williamson; the Sewanee Writers' Conference; Teach Living Poets, LNCS and Melissa Alter Smith.

Salamat to Mom & Dad, my family, and the Mahjong Crew, who will always have my heart—and who will always be home.

And to Jennifer, Xavier, and Penelope: *I love you more than everything.*

RECENT TITLES FROM ALICE JAMES BOOKS

The Palace, Andrés Cerpa
Let the Moon Wobble, Ally Ang
The Seeds, Cecily Parks
All the Possible Bodies, Iain Haley Pollock
Saint Consequence, Michael M. Weinstein
Freeland, Leigh Sugar
Mothersalt, Mia Ayumi Malhotra
When the Horses, Mary Helen Callier
Cold Thief Place, Esther Lin
If Nothing, Matthew Nienow
Zombie Vomit Mad Libs, Duy Đoàn
The Holy & Broken Bliss, Alicia Ostriker
Wish Ave, Alessandra Lynch
Autobiomythography of, Ayokunle Falomo
Old Stranger: Poems, Joan Larkin
I Don't Want To Be Understood, Joshua Jennifer Espinoza
Canandaigua, Donald Revell
In the Days That Followed, Kevin Goodan
Light Me Down: The New & Collected Poems of Jean Valentine, Jean Valentine
Song of My Softening, Omotara James
Theophanies, Sarah Ghazal Ali
Orders of Service, Willie Lee Kinard III
The Dead Peasant's Handbook, Brian Turner
The Goodbye World Poem, Brian Turner
The Wild Delight of Wild Things, Brian Turner
I Am the Most Dangerous Thing, Candace Williams
Burning Like Her Own Planet, Vandana Khanna
Standing in the Forest of Being Alive, Katie Farris
Feast, Ina Cariño
Decade of the Brain: Poems, Janine Joseph
American Treasure, Jill McDonough
We Borrowed Gentleness, J. Estanislao Lopez
Brother Sleep, Aldo Amparán
Sugar Work, Katie Marya

Alice James Books is committed to publishing books that matter. The press was founded in 1973 in Boston, Massachusetts to give women access to publishing. As a cooperative, authors performed the day-to-day undertakings of the press. The press continues to expand and grow from its formative roots, guided by its founding values of access, excellence, inclusivity, and collaboration in publishing. Its mission is to publish books that matter and preserve a place of belonging for poets who inspire us. AJB seeks to broaden our collective interpretation of what constitutes the American poetic voice and is dedicated to helping its artists achieve purposeful engagement with broad audiences and communities nationwide. The press was named for Alice James, sister to William and Henry, whose extraordinary gift for writing went unrecognized during her lifetime.

Designed by Tiani Kennedy
Printed by Versa Press